Shattered:

BECOMING ONE

CIELLE H.

Published in the United States by The Velvet Society Publishing.
First edition, 2025.

Cover design by Cielle H.
Interior layout by Cielle H.

For inquiries, permissions, or rights, contact:
thevelvetsocietypublishing@gmail.com

ISBN: [To be added upon registration]

Printed in the United States of America

Dedication

To the girl who survived what no one saw—
and the woman she became in the quiet after.

This is for the you that kept breathing, even when
you forgot how.

PAGE LEFT INTENTIONALLY BLANK

Contents

PAGE LEFT INTENTIONALLY BLANK

Authors Note

I didn't write this book to bleed.
I wrote it to remember who I was before the break—
and to gather the pieces I've reclaimed since.

There are names I'll never speak,
nights I'll never forget.
But this book is not about them.

It's about what rose from the wreckage.
It's about becoming whole without needing to be perfect.
It's about telling the truth—softly, sharply—
so it can never be stolen again.

These pages are breath, offered one inhale at a time.

Some poems rhyme. Others don't.
That's intentional.

Rhyme gave me rhythm when I needed structure.
Free verse gave me breath when I needed space.

Healing is like that—sometimes melodic, sometimes messy.
Some pieces whisper. Others roar.
But all of them are real.

I didn't write to be poetic.
I wrote to be free.

— Cielle H.

PAGE LEFT INTENTIONALLY BLANK

Fracture

The moment it broke. The before-and-after. The crack you couldn't unhear.

First Lie

The first lie I learned
was to smile on cue—
to nod, to agree,
to keep the peace
even as it cost me mine.

I became so good
at wearing that face
I forgot it was a mask
until it cracked.

I swallowed my questions,
bit down my rage,
made myself smaller
to fit in their frame.

They called it respect,
called it being good—
but it was surrender
in a borrowed hood.

It took years to unlearn
what they called love—
to let my own voice
rise up, unshoved.

Now I see the lie
for what it was:
a prison dressed
as belonging.

And I won't go back.

Inheritance

I learned silence far too young,
how to bite my restless tongue—
swallow truth and wear a grin,
keep the chaos locked within.

Called it love and loyalty,
called it keeping harmony—
but all it was, beneath the gloss,
was fear disguised as lesser loss.

Smiles that never reached my eyes,
words I learned to memorize—
polished lies we passed along,
taught that quiet made us strong.

It took years to count the cost,
the voice I buried, the self I lost—
the way the secrets turned to stone,
a burden carved into my bones.

I won't wear this borrowed shame,
won't play the old inheritance game—
I lay it down, I end the line,
this silent legacy isn't mine.

What Did I Do to Deserve This?

I searched the stars for some offense,
A reason why it made no sense.
Was I too soft, too loud, too kind?
Was guilt the bruise you hoped to find?

I traced each step, replayed the fall,
As if my worth explained it all.
I begged the silence for a sign—
But pain, it speaks in crooked lines.

I wore the blame like borrowed skin,
As if your harm came from within.
But love, real love, would never twist
And leave me drowning in a fist.

So here's the truth I came to see:
There's nothing wrong inside of me.
What I "deserved" was care and peace,
Not gaslit nights or joy on lease.

I did not earn that ache you gave.
I am not something you could save.
I am a light you tried to dim—
But I still rise, with every limb.

The Memory I Wish I Didn't Have

It visits me in silence loud,
In shadow's edge, beneath the shroud.
A touch, a word, a quiet stare—
A weight I carry unaware.

It wasn't sharp, it wasn't fast,
But slow, like dusk that lingers past.
It crawled beneath my guarded skin,
And marked the space where trust had been.

A joke, a glance, a shift of air—
I didn't know what wasn't fair.
Until my body screamed inside,
While I just smiled and let it slide.

I wish it didn't live so deep,
This scar I tend, this ache I keep.
But even wounds I try to hide
Still pulse with truth I can't deny.

So I'll forgive what won't forget,
And honor pain with no regret.
The girl who flinched and didn't speak—
She was the brave one. She was me.

You Got to Sleep at Night

You closed your eyes like nothing cracked,
Like silence stitched what you attacked.
While I lay haunted, torn, and bruised—
You dreamt with ease, your conscience snoozed.

You sipped your lies like vintage wine,
Let shadows cloak what you called fine.
But truth has teeth and time keeps score—
The pain you dodged knocks at your door.

You rested while I begged for air,
While I replayed the vacant stare.
But now I see—your peace was fake,
A cover for the harm you'd make.

So sleep, if sleep is what you claim,
But know your dreams still speak my name.
And if you toss, or flinch, or cry—
It's not revenge, it's truth that's nigh.

For every night I could not rest,
You tucked your lies into your chest.
But now I rise—your mask, undone.
I've faced the dark. I am the sun.

Fatal Attraction

He spoke like velvet, eyes like wine,
A practiced charm, a worn-out line.
He drew me close with practiced ease,
A whisper dressed in false appease.

He laughed too loud, then stared too long,
I knew the notes, but missed the song.
He said he'd stay, then disappeared,
Turned sweet to sharp when I came near.

It wasn't love—it was control,
A puppet act to claim my soul.
He touched my waist like it was owed,
Then left me heavy with the load.

The fire burned but brought no light,
Just smoke that choked me every night.
What pulled me in was not his face—
But hope that I could change his pace.

But I've outlived that cruel refrain,
I know the dance, I've felt the chain.
No more illusions, no more ache—
True love won't make your spirit break

REFLECTION:

This is the Moment Everything Changed

The shattering didn't begin with screaming. It began with silence—the kind that echoed long after the door shut. This is where the story split, where breath became jagged, and where time became a before and after. This section holds the scream I couldn't let out and the fear that made a home in my ribs. I did not imagine what was done to me. This was real. This was the beginning.

AFFIRMATIONS:

I am not broken—I am breaking through.

What happened to me is not who I am.

Even in silence, I was still sacred.

PAGE LEFT INTENTIONALLY BLANK

Fragments

Memory scattered. Relationships misaligned.
The questions that don't quiet.

Innocence

He saw an angel,
Her pureness made him feel worse,
He had an angle,
He wanted her to be cursed,
The innocence in her heart,
Her innocent mind,
Her willingness to love him,
The desire to stay blind,
To the coldness of others,
and To losing all trust,
He saw an angel that day,
Then he left her in the dust.

Chosen

Ever want to be chosen,
Not lied to and broken,
Told the timing was bad,
Still looked at like a token,
Ever want to be loved,
Like no one ever was,
Not favored for the moment,
Then left when push came to shove,
Ever needed someones word,
To match all of their actions,
To be told "I miss you",
Not second guess their antics,
Ever tired of waiting,
To get an ounce of admiration,
From someone who shows,
they truly have no concentration,
Im tired of the words,
Tired of the false promises,
I just want to be chosen,
I just need some acknowledgment,
My heart is going numb,
I heard it too many times,
"You're the one that got away,
I wasn't ready at the time".

The Bare Minimum Felt Like Love

I called it romance
when he replied.
Settled for presence
when he barely tried.

I thought silence was comfort—
it was distance, in disguise.
Mistook his coldness
for depth behind his eyes.

He gave me crumbs,
and I built feasts.
Took broken moments
and called them peace.

Clapped for gestures
he should've just given.
Called longing devotion—
but it was survival, not living.

I stretched myself thin
for a maybe, a chance.
I bent into versions
he might glance at twice.

But I won't go back.

I don't fault the girl
who loved with all her might—
I just won't starve again
for a man who feared the light.

Pitch Black

He looks in her eyes,
She looks at her lap,
She's nervous, what will happen?
She knows it's a trap,
She gives of herself,
And the two souls mingle,
They flow with each other,
They don't want to be single,
But after it's all done,
And the covers kickback,
Her soul walks away,
And his doesn't look back.
She has nothing left,
She gave it all away,
She wanted him to feel her love,
She wanted it to stay,
The cycle continues,
She's on to the next,
Who else will she meet?
Her soul is pitch black.

The Tired Ritual

Late-night scrolls and endless streams,
Trading sleep for brittle dreams—
A thousand ways to hush the ache,
To quiet thoughts I couldn't shake.

Distractions dressed in sweet disguise,
Soft escapes and borrowed highs—
Habits wrapped around my heart,
A way to tear the dark apart.

Every vice a fleeting claim,
A promise I could not sustain—
But morning always found me bare,
The hollow cost too much to bear.

I'm learning now to feel it all,
To catch my tears before they fall—
To stand unguarded in the rain,
And love the marrow of my pain.

The Time of Day

Why did I give you the time of day?
You wasted my energy,
and You made me pay,
In kisses, in hugs, and in many other ways,
I gave of myself,
and still have nothing to say.
Remember I'm special,
I teach you some things,
Too bad there's only one thing you ever
taught me,
It's that sympathy won't get me very far
honestly,
and its sympathy that's breaking down my
heart, tragically.
Now I'm tired and uninterested,
Im over the back and forth,
One question for you though,
Can I get back the time I put forth?

Potential

I always sit and wonder,
what it is that I see,
I pay attention,
I look close,
I try and learn everything
I go beyond the first layer,
I imagine what could be,
If I just take a chance,
Or if I just wait and see,
But what do I get?
Some wasted time,
Few unread texts,
Because I saw potential,
I ignored everything,
He liked me for some time,
Till I was too hard to decieve,
Now I don't see potential,
I see distant memories.

Benefit of Doubt

The benefit of doubt
Gave so much I can't keep count
You listening to their heart
They busy shooting words out the mouth
I tried to understand the why from the what
Started to self sacrifice to help mend your heart
You pushed and pushed then it all went away
You don't want to be heard
You don't want me to stay
You want to turn me out
Make me in your image
 make me less devout
Change me so I fit in
Take away my empathy
Leave me less than sound
Make me cold and numb like the other ppl around
I won't stop loving the people I have around me,
and I won't let you win , even if you doubt me.

REFLECTION:

What Trauma Does to Memory

Trauma doesn't always leave a scar you can point to. It buries
itself in fragments—flashes, sensations, the way your body
flinches at nothing. This section holds what I tried to forget
but couldn't. Not because I was weak, but because my body
kept the score. I've learned memory is not linear—it is
layered, and every layer deserves compassion.

AFFIRMATIONS:

I believe what my body remembers.

I do not need their validation to honor my truth.

Each piece of memory I reclaim is a victory.

PAGE LEFT INTENTIONALLY BLANK

Rage and Reckoning

*The fire you were told to snuff. The
clarity that came with heat.*

Mark My Words

I won't shrink again to fit a space I've outgrown.
Won't silence my knowing to soothe your comfort zone.

I used to whisper truth like it was sin.
Now I speak it in full volume—
no edits, no grin.

You underestimated a woman mid-rise,
called me dramatic when I dared analyze
the cracks in your mask,
the script you rehearsed.
You played the victim—
I played it worse:
The girl who stayed silent,
who blamed herself first.

But no more.
I'm not your echo,
your cushion,
your cure.
I am thunder,
with receipts.
Watch me roar—
secure.

Benefit of Doubt

I gave you the benefit of doubt
like it was candy—sweet and cheap.
Told myself you meant well
as I rocked myself to sleep.

Excused the tone.
Defended the mood.
Said, "He's just tired."
Swallowed the rude.

But every time I gave you grace,
you filled that space
with your own face.
Made it about you.
Made me small.
Until one day—
I stopped the fall.

Now doubt is a gift I give with care,
not something you get just because you were there.

Pitch Black

sharper focus, deeper impact, stronger close

It went pitch black before it got better.
Silence held me tighter than any lover.
My voice, a whisper I couldn't hear—
my body, a map etched in fear.

They say healing is light,
but they don't talk about the night.
About screaming without sound,
about pacing holy ground
trying to feel God
in a room that stayed still.

But still—
I rose.

Not because of strength,
but in spite of pain.
Because something inside me
refused to stay the same.

Pitch black couldn't hold me,
though it tried with both hands.
Now I glow by choice—
not demand.

Rewrite My Past / Forgiving Myself

I used to beg for time to bend,
To rewrite scenes I couldn't mend.
To wish away each silent scream,
To edit out each shattered dream.

I'd hold the past like broken glass,
And bleed while watching moments pass.
I'd pray to change the paths I took,
The lines I wrote in every look.

But now I know, the goal's not clean—
It's not to wipe the pages clean.
It's learning how to hold the scar,
And still believe in who you are.

Forgiveness starts with gentle grace,
A softened voice, a slower pace.
To hold that girl who stayed too long,
And tell her: none of it was wrong.

She did her best, she gave her all,
She stood up every time the fall.
No more regret, no need to flee—
The past is past, but I am me.

Standards

"You're so pretty, you're so smart"
I see you even have a heart,"
You have a man? You need a friend?"
I tend to think that all depends,
On what you have for me,
Because my love is not for free,
and I'm not getting that same feeling
The one you say you have for me,
You see my face,
you hear my thoughts,
You're shocked and very impressed,
But sadly when I look at you,
I see my future regrets,
Am I wrong to have standards?
Am I wrong to disagree?
The vision you have for US,
The Same vision I don't see,
They say everybody has somebody,
But babe,
Your someone isn't me.

Too Good

She was too good for him,
She knew it at first glance,
He wanted whoever he could get,
Whoever gave him a chance,
She saw past his front,
Even saw past the ego,
She saw he had a heart,
She saw it even through the evil,
He made her hurt,
He made her cry,
Made her ask herself why,
She taught him life,
He learned a lot,
She was what he "wanted",
But she was way too good,
Oh well She won't be taunted.

When I Bit My Tongue

I swallowed whole hurricanes
to keep peace.
Choked on silence
so no one else had to flinch.

But rage is not a tantrum—
it's evidence.
A scar speaking in present tense.

When I bit my tongue,
I bled truth.
Now I speak
and watch the room shift.

REFLECTION:

The Sharp Edge of Clarity

Anger isn't the enemy—shame is. For too long, I swallowed my voice to keep the peace. This section is what happens when I stop shrinking. When I choose myself. When I stop editing my rage to make others comfortable. The fire was never a flaw. It was the beginning of my power.

AFFIRMATIONS:

My anger is not a weakness—it's a warning and a witness.

I do not owe silence to anyone who harmed me.

I am allowed to outgrow those who kept me small.

Return

When softness stops being weakness.
When your no becomes sacred.

Chameleon Skin

I tried on every shade they wore,
Soft pastels and something more—
Changed my colors, changed my tone,
Hid the truth I called my own.

I curved my edges, played the part,
Learned the script by practiced heart—
But quiet nights would always show,
The self I thought they'd never know.

I am not their borrowed line,
Not a shape that must align—
I am vivid, I am free,
An anthem no one else can be.

Let them whisper, let them spin,
I was never meant to blend in—
Born to stand where few will go,
A song that only I can know.

Panther

They thought I'd return soft,
pliable,
begging for crumbs.

But I came back
with velvet claws
and eyes that didn't flinch.

I move silent now,
but not scared.
I've learned
that power doesn't always roar—
sometimes it purrs,
sometimes it walks alone,
sometimes it waits in the dark
and strikes only when it's ready.

Call it rage.
Call it rebirth.
Call it the panther in me
that survived.

The Quietest Victory

It didn't look like fireworks—
no grand exit, no crowd.
Just me,
walking away from what I once begged for.

I didn't slam a door.
I didn't scream.
I just left.

And in that stillness,
I heard something holy—
my own breath,
uninterrupted.

Unfollowed

He used to watch my stories
like a ghost checking the window
of the house he burned.

For a while,
I liked the attention—
like survival had an audience.

But I don't need haunted applause.
I need clean air.

So I closed the curtains.
Removed the eyes.
And in the quiet,
I remembered how it feels
to see myself.

Dear Future Me

I hope you wake with gentler thoughts,
Not haunted by the battles fought.
I hope your smile comes soft and wide,
No longer needing masks to hide.

I hope the mirror shows your grace,
Not every scar you had to face.
I hope your past feels far, not near,
And peace has dulled what once was fear.

I hope you love with steady hands,
With roots grown deep like sacred lands.
I hope you walk where sunlight plays,
And rest becomes your holy praise.

I hope you never shrink or bend
To make the lonely feel like friends.
I hope your "no" rings loud and true,
And guilt no longer lives in you.

You are the woman I became
When I stepped out of loss and shame.
I hope you hold that truth with pride—
You lived, you healed, you did not hide.

Pure Gold

Now I see when they said,
"You don't want to be old",
This struggle to maintain,
That was never my goal.
I craved things to do,
I wanted people to see,
But never took into account,
All of that isn't everything.
The days that pass,
and the memories I make,
Experiences that seem to keep shaping my face,
I'm happy for them all,
I know this to be true,
There's just something on my mind,
Maybe this applies to you too,
Constant battles to be won,
Many lessons to be learned,
I keep on shapeshifting,
Change at every single turn,
This journey called life,
I know I'll be alright,
Because I'm pure gold,
I shine even in the night.

A *Letter to My Younger Self*

Sweet girl,
You were never too much.
They just didn't know how to hold your light
without dimming it to survive.

I wish you knew
your softness wasn't a flaw—
it was a language the world hadn't learned yet.

I see you,
sitting quiet in your room,
wondering if anyone hears your heart
when it breaks in secret.

I hear it now.
I honor it now.
And I promise:
we made it.
Not untouched—
but undefeated.

You didn't disappear,
you transformed.
And I carry you now
in every brave thing I do.

REFLECTION:

The Sharp Edge of Clarity

Anger isn't the enemy—shame is. For too long, I swallowed my voice to keep the peace. This section is what happens when I stop shrinking. When I choose myself. When I stop editing my rage to make others comfortable. The fire was never a flaw. It was the beginning of my power.

AFFIRMATIONS:

My anger is not a weakness—it's a warning and a witness.

I do not owe silence to anyone who harmed me.

I am allowed to outgrow those who kept me small.

One

Wholeness is not going back—it's carrying it all, beautifully.

No Longer Waiting

I used to ache for follow-through—
for someone to mean it
when they said, "I'm here for you."

But I've learned:
some promises are petals—
soft,
but never rooted.
Pretty words that wilt
the moment you reach for them.

Now,
I hold my own hand
when the world gets loud.
I build my quiet
without needing to be found.

I've stopped keeping score
of who didn't stay.
I stay.
That's enough.

You don't need to show up anymore.
I already did.

What I Know Now

I used to think love had to ache,
That worth was proved by what you'd take.
I dimmed my light to make them stay,
But silence doesn't keep wolves at bay.

I thought "I'm sorry" made it right,
That second chances cleared the night.
But now I know a heart must mend—
Not bend itself to just pretend.

I know now peace is not a prize
You beg for underneath closed eyes.
It's something claimed in quiet breath,
When you no longer flirt with death.

I know that walking out is grace,
That boundaries build a sacred space.
And loving me means holding true—
Not breaking me to carry you.

I'm not too much, I'm not too loud.
My fire was never meant to bow.
What I know now could fill the sky—
And still, it grows each time I cry.

Unboxed

Don't ask me to fit
in your tidy frame—
to quiet my fire,
to shrink my flame.

I am too layered
to be explained,
too wild, too vivid
to be restrained.

Call me too much—
I'll call it true.
Better unbound
than easy for you.

I won't shrink down
to soothe your fear.
I was never small—
I'm crystal clear.

I am a marvel—
unboxed and free,
remarkable, whole,
exactly me.

Arrival

No parade,
no applause—
just the quiet knowing
that I made it here.

I am not unbroken,
but I am unafraid.

I call this wholeness—
not perfection,
but finally
belonging to myself.

I used to think healing
would feel like triumph,
like a banner raised
over every scar.

But it feels more like breathing—
like waking up
and realizing
I don't need permission
to be complete.

No one else had to witness it.
No one else had to name it.

It was enough
that I arrived.

I Am the After

I am not who they left.
Not what they bruised.
Not the sum of the nights
I was silenced or used.

I am the after.
The bloom beyond harm.
The breath after drowning.
The calm after alarm.

They don't get to name me.
Not anymore.
I've renamed my reflection
and rebuilt the floor.

I walk taller now,
not because I'm unscarred—
but because I stitched those scars
into stories,
into stars.

I don't need your approval.
I don't beg to be seen.
I am no one's wound now—
I am queen.

Celebrating My Survival

I celebrate not the pain—
but the passage.
Not the storm—
but the stillness I earned after.

This survival is not an apology.
It is a song,
a scream,
a sunrise with my name on it.

I don't just exist—
I declare.
I don't just breathe—
I blaze.

They tried to end me.
But here I am,
unfolding like fire
in a field that once buried me.

I lived.
I live.
And that alone
deserves a crown.

Concrete Bloom

In the cracks they never see,
A quiet seed took hold of me—
No promise here of gentle ground,
No gardener's hand to wrap me round.

I grew beneath a sky of stone,
My roots unseen, my will alone—
Petals blushed in spite of scars,
Reaching up to kiss the stars.

They called me fragile, doomed to fade,
A bloom that time would soon degrade—
But still I rise, defy decay,
A rose that blooms her own fierce way.

So let them doubt what they can't feel,
I am the proof, the wound that heals—
A miracle they can't unsee,
A rose that cracked the concrete free.

REFLECTION:

The Day I Chose Myself

Coming back to myself wasn't loud. It was in the no I said without apologizing. In the softness I reclaimed without guilt. I learned that peace is power. That my body is mine. And that healing isn't a straight line—it's a spiral, and I am allowed to dance in the curve.

AFFIRMATIONS:

My boundaries are holy.

Softness is not surrender—it is my revolution.

I can be gentle and still take up space.

About The Author

Cielle H. is a poet, survivor, and soft architect of truth.

Her work explores healing after trauma, feminine resilience, and the sacred power of saying no more.

Shattered: Becoming One is her debut poetry collection—a hybrid of poems, prose, and spiritual reclamation.

She is the founder of Glow Era Society, a digital print boutique rooted in self-worth, mystique, and emotional intelligence.

www.ingramcontent.com/pod-product-compliance
Lightning Source LLC
Chambersburg PA
CBHW030222140626
46545CB00012B/2850